COMPI...

T0282227

LITTLE BOOK OF
NEVILLE GODDARD
QUOTES

THE POCKET GUIDE TO MYSTICISM,
MANIFESTATION & IMAGINATION

MUSE
ORACLE
PRESS

TABLE OF CONTENTS

INTRODUCTION

Awakening The Kingdom Within By Jen Mccarty

Deep within the recesses of our being lies an extraordinary power, an awe-inspiring force that holds the key to understanding the universe and our place in it.

This power, often overlooked and underestimated, is the kingdom of heaven within us—the perfect power of our imagination. Just as a fractal mirrors the whole, our imagination reflects a fragmented yet divine aspect of the mind of God.

Imagination is not just a realm of childish fantasies or idle daydreams; it is the very seat of eternal consciousness that accompanies us throughout our journey on this earthly plane. When these mortal vessels fade away, the essence of our imagination remains, connecting us to a profound spiritual reality.

It is the kingdom of heaven within, the mind of God dwelling within each and every one of us.

Ancient scriptures and sacred teachings have long hinted at the significance of this power. The Bible, in particular, reveals that the imagination is symbolised as the "Father".

In its profound verse. "I and my Father are one," this is a proclamation that our conscious mind houses the same boundless creative potential that the Almighty possesses.

In embracing this understanding, we recognise that we are co-creators with the divine, endowed with the ability to bring forth realities through the wondrous faculties of our imagination.

The process of creation, it turns out, begins within the realm of the imagination. Every aspect of our world, from the towering structures we build to the intricate tapestries of our lives, originates from the vivid landscapes of our inner thoughts. The paradisical consciousness within us is a wellspring of unconditional creativity, just waiting to be tapped into and unleashed.

As we find ourselves in this moment of profound collective awakening, we are called to remember who we truly are, to connect with the boundless potential residing within our perfect imagination. It is a journey of self-discovery that leads us to realise the truth: our imagination is the true reality. It is the wellspring from which all things flow, the very essence of our existence.

In the pages that follow, we will delve into the profound teachings of Neville Goddard, a luminary who illuminated the path to harnessing the power of imagination. His wisdom and insights will guide us on a transformative journey, as we awaken to the divinity that lies within. Together, we will explore the depths of our creative essence, unlocking the secrets of the universe and the connection to the mind of God. Through this awakening, we will find the means to shape our destinies, to manifest dreams into reality, and to embrace the profound responsibility of co-creating with the divine.

As we embark on this journey, let us remember that the kingdom of heaven is not a distant realm beyond our reach; it is a sacred space within us, waiting to be discovered and cherished. Through the power of imagination, we will unlock the gateway to the divine within, stepping into a reality where dreams become tangible, and the ordinary transcends into the extraordinary.

Within the realm of our perfect imagination lies a profound truth—when we embrace the transformative power of the words "I am" and comprehend the magnitude of these words, we gain the ability to script the very narrative of our lives. As we align our consciousness with the desires of the "I am," a resounding chorus of hallelujahs echoes through every member of our soul group. The "I am" state represents the highest vibratory state in existence, and when one individual within the soul group awakens to their "I am" presence, a ripple effect of elevation cascades through the entire collective. Each soul, in turn, is empowered to realise their oneness with their "I am" presence swiftly and harmoniously.

In this state of interconnectedness, all that we could ever desire is already within reach, awaiting only to be matched by the beliefs we hold. The power to manifest our dreams lies not in some distant horizon but within the very core of our being. Our beliefs become the architects of our reality, shaping the outcomes of our experiences and transforming the mundane into the extraordinary.

As we embark on this journey of self- discovery and connection with the mind of God through our imagination, let us remember the potency of the words "I am." Embrace them, understand them, and wield them with intent, for they are the keys that unlock the hidden potential within us. The awakening of the "I am" presence has the power to uplift not only ourselves but our entire soul group, exponentially supporting each individualised member on their path towards oneness with their divine essence.

In the chapters that follow, we will delve deeper into the teachings of Neville Goddard, exploring the profound significance of the "I am" state and the principles that govern the art of conscious creation. This journey will reveal the innate wisdom and creative prowess that lies dormant within each of us, awaiting our recognition and activation.

The time of great collective awakening is upon us, and the kingdom of heaven within awaits our exploration. The gateway to our true reality is not some distant destination; it is within our grasp, within the very fabric of our imagination and consciousness. As we learn to harness the power of the "I am," we will embark on a transformative odyssey, rediscovering our purpose, awakening our creative potential, and stepping into the truth of who we are meant to be.

When you realise that you are the sole operative power in the universe, you fully awaken to God consciousness. As God consciousness, you are never a victim of circumstances; you are always in creator mode. True enlightenment and awakening involve understanding that your individualised subjective experience is like a hologram, where you are the writer, actor, director, and producer. If there are characters in your hologram that are not participating in alignment with your preferences, you must shift your internal attitude toward these situations and relationships, and observe how that manifests in the third-dimensional realm.

God source energy can only create complete fractals of itself. When we grasp this concept, we understand that we are all individualised fragments of wholeness, and therefore, we are the masters of our own conscious movie experience. In a movie, the producer has the power to create characters according to their desired scene development.

However, the insidious programming of the lower dimensions has sought to hypnotise us into forgetting this monumental truth. There is only one operative power in the universe, and that is the I AM Presence. What the I AM Presence sees and perceives is what it will experience in the lower third-dimensional realms.

This is the pinnacle of awakening, when one can finally step into the higher spiritual garments of their angelic I AM Presence and navigate this earthly realm, fully awakened to the understanding and inner standing of their unique power to subjectively co-create heaven on Earth, also referred to as paradise or Zion.

Understanding that there is no other, is the ultimate key to spiritual liberation. If you are attached to the lower-dimensional realms, you may believe in the power and free will of others. However, this level of understanding is a stage toward ultimately remembering who you are as the I AM Presence.

There is only one I AM Presence, and we are all fragments of that I AM Presence. Nothing and no one is separate from the I AM Presence, nor can they ever be separated. Thus, we awaken to the realisation that our subjective experience of reality precisely creates reality, and this applies to all aspects of our lives.

In my humble opinion, Neville Goddard is the greatest mystic that has ever lived and it has taken me many years of being on a spiritual enlightenment path to truly understand Neville's teachings. Open your heart now to receive these powerful hand-picked quotes from Neville's work.

These quotes will help open your heart and expand your consciousness and guide you back home to full remembrance and embodiment of your I am presence.

Welcome to the awakening of the kingdom within. Let the journey begin.

THE IMAGINATION

The spirit of God in you is your imagination but it sleeps and needs to be awakened in order to lift you off the ball of the senses where you have so long laid stranded.

Imagination is the very gateway to reality.

The real man, the imaginative man, has invested the outer world with all of its properties.
The apparent reality of the outer world, which is so hard to dissolve, is only proof of the absolute reality of the inner world of his own imagination.

Behold, though it appears without, it is within, in your imagination, of which this world of mortality is but a mere shadow.

Blake, Jerusalem

The first power that meets us at the threshold of the soul's domain is the power of imagination.

Dr. Franz Hartmann

The moment man discovers that his imagination is Christ, he accomplishes his acts, which, on this level, can only be called miraculous.

It is a marvelous thing to discover that you can imagine yourself into the state of your fulfilled desire and escape from the traps that ignorance has built. The real man is a magnificent imagination, and it is this self that must be awakened.

The imaginative man does not deny the reality of the sensuous outer world of becoming, but he knows that it is the inner world of continuous imagination that is the force by which the sensuous outer world of becoming comes to pass. He sees the outer world and all its happenings as projections of the inner world of imagination.

Truth depends upon the intensity of the imagination, not solely upon external facts. Facts or outcomes bear witness to the use or misuse of imagination.

Where the natural man of senses sees something bad, the imaginative person sees a rose.

As we awaken to the imaginative life, we realize that to imagine a thing is to make it so. A true judgment need not always conform to the external reality to which it relates.

Only awakened imagination can enter into and partake of the nature of its opposite.

Truth depends upon the intensity of the imagination, not upon external facts.

As we awaken to the imaginative life, we discover that to imagine a thing is to make it so. A true judgement need not conform to the external reality to which it relates.

It is a marvellous thing to find that you can imagine yourself into the state of your fulfilled desire and escape from the guiles that ignorance built. The real man is a magnificent imagination, and it is this self that must be awakened.

Somewhere within this realm of imagination, there is a mood, a feeling of the wish fulfilled, which, if appropriated, means success to you, this realm, this Eden, your imagination is vaster than you know and deserves exploration.

If you do not control your imagination, your imagination will control you. Whatever you confidently suggest becomes law to the subject of the mind; it is under obligation to objectify that which we affirm. Not only does the subject execute the state, but he does it as though the decision had come of itself or the idea had originated from him.

We are made subject to the limitations of the senses and clothed in bodies of flesh to train us in image making.

Imagine yourself to be the ideal you dream of and desire. Remain attentive to this imagined state, and as far as you feel entirely that you are already this ideal, it will manifest itself as reality in your world.

Your imagination is able to do all that you ask in proportion to the degree of your attention. All the progress, and all the fulfilment of desire depend upon the control and concentration of your attention.

Imagination and faith are the secrets
of creation.

Imagination is the beginning of creation.
You imagine what you desire, and then believe it to be true. Every dream can be realised by those self-disciplined enough to believe it, people are what you choose to make them. A man is according to the manner in which you look at him. You must look at him with different eyes before he will objectively change.

EVERYONE IS YOU
POPPED OUT

Man must firmly come to believe that reality lies within him, and not without, although others have bodies, a life of their own, their reality is rooted in you.

What you truly believe with others you will awaken within them.
The vibratory state transmitted by your belief persists until it awakens its corresponding vibration in him of whom it is believed.

THINKING FROM THE END

Thinking from the state desired is creative living, ignorance of this ability to think from the end is bondage.

Determined imagination, thinking from the end is the beginning of all miracles.

To passively surrender to the evidence of the senses, underestimates the capacities of the inner self.

You who know this law will find that after capturing the psychological state, which would be yours if you were already victoriously and securely entrenched in that city or state, you will move towards the physical realisation of your desires. You will do this without doubt or fear, in a state of mind fixed in the knowledge of a pre-arranged victory.

We must use imagination, masterfully, not as an onlooker thinking of the end, but as a partaker thinking from the end, we must actually be there in imagination. If we do this, our subjective experience will be realised objectively.

Thinking from the end is the way of Christ.

Determined imagination, thinking from the end is the beginning of all miracles.

BIBLICAL QUOTES

Wherever the sole of your foot shall tread, the same give I onto you.

Joshua 13

Unless a man is born again, he cannot enter the kingdom of God.

John 3:3

No man takes it from me, but I lay it down of myself.

John 10:17-18

The kingdom of heaven is within you.

Luke 17:12

Matching the beliefs of a state is the seeking that finds and is the asking that receives.

Matthew 7:8

If I do not do the works of my Father, do not believe me; but if I do them, though you do not believe me, believe the works, that you may know and believe that the Father is in me and I am in him.

John 10:37-38

My father and I are one.

John 10:30

My word shall not return onto me void, it shall prosper in the thing where to I sent it.

Isaiah 55:11.

And remember the Lord thy God in the midst of thee is mighty.

Zephaniah, 3:17

Choose this day whom you will serve.

Joshua 24:15

And now, Father, glorify me in your presence with the glory I had with you before the world began.

John 17:5

My house shall be called a house of prayer for all people.

Isaiah 56, 7

The father's consciousness has ways that no man knows. It is the unanswerable law.

Romans 11:33

There is only one way that which you seek can enter your world: I am the door.

John 10:9

What things soever you desire when you pray, believe that you receive them, and you shall receive them.

Mark 11.24

The kingdom of heaven is within you.

Luke 17:12

Two shall agree as touching anything and it shall be established on.

Matthew 18:19

Now you will see the wisdom in the words of the prophet. When he states let the weak say I am strong.

Joel, 3:10

I am the light of the world.

John 8:12

Shut the door, pray to the Father, who is in secret, and the Father, who sees in secret, shall reward you openly.

Matthew 6:6

Man lives not by bread alone, but by every word that proceeds out of the mouth of God.

Matthew 4:4,

Let this mind be in you, which was also in Christ Jesus, who, being in the form of God, thought it not robbery to be equal with God.

Philippians, 25:6.

Call those things which be not as though they were.

Romans 4:17

Son, thou art ever with me and all that I have is thine.

Luke 15:31

And the Lord God caused a deep sleep to fall upon Adam and he slept.

Genesis 2:21

But when you pray, go into your room, close the door and pray to your Father, who is unseen. Then your Father, who sees what is done in secret, will reward you.

Matthew 6:6

Closing the door of the senses is not as difficult as it appears to be. At first. It is done without effort. It is impossible to serve two masters at the same time.

Matthew 6:24,

INNER SPEECH

Observe your inner speech, for it is the cause of future action. Inner speech reveals the state of consciousness, from which you view the world. Make your inner speech match your fulfilled desire for your inner speech is manifested all around you in happenings, thus making one born again.

The present moment is always precisely right for an investment to speak the right word inwardly.

Right inner speech is essential. It is the greatest of the arts.

Does your inner talking match what you would
say audibly had you achieved your goal?

God has bestowed two gifts upon mankind alone, distinguishing them from other mortal creatures: the gifts of mind and speech. These gifts are equivalent to the gift of immortality. If a person uses these two gifts wisely, they will be no different from the Immortals. When they leave their physical body, the mind and speech will be their guides, leading them to the truth of the gods, and their souls will attain bliss in the hermetic realm.

We cannot abandon the moment to negative inner talking and be expected to retain command of life.

What we desire does not lie in the future, but in ourselves at this very moment.

THOUGHTS

Thought is the Queen of heaven. Money is its earthly symbol.

Everything we do unaccompanied by a change of consciousness is but a futile readjustment of surfaces. However much we toil and struggle, we can receive no more than our concept of self allows.

To protest against anything that happens to us is to protest against the law of our being and to shipwreck our own destiny.

HERMES

The world, says Hermes is the son, and the mind is father of the word.
They are not separate one from the other, for life is the union of word and mind.

Life said Hermes is the union of words and mind. When imagination matches your inner speech in accordance with your fulfilled desire, there will then be a shift in yourself from within, and the without will instantly reflect the within, and you will know the reality is only actualised in our inner speech.

Hermes tells us the future must become the present in the imagination of the one who would wisely and consciously create circumstances.

SELF CONCEPT

I cannot change another unless I first change myself. To change another within my world, I must first change my concept of that other, and to do it best, I change my concept of self. For it was the concept I held of self that made me see others as I did.

My concept of myself molds a world in harmony with itself and draws people to constantly reflect who I am through their behavior.

We are what we imagine we are.

There is no reality in the world other than your self concept.

When men and women help or hinder us, they only play the part that we, by our concept of self, wrote for them, and they play it automatically. They must play the parts they are playing because we are what we are.

You will change the world only when you become the embodiment of that which you want the world to be. You have got one gift in this world that is truly yours to give, and that is yourself. Unless you give yourself all that which you want the world to be, you will never see it in this world. Except you believe not that I am he, he shall die in your sins.

Any enlargement of our concept of self involves some pain, as we part with strongly rooted hereditary conceptions. The ligaments that hold us in the womb of conventional limitations are strong. All that you once believed, you no longer believe.
You now know that there is no power outside of your own consciousness; therefore, you cannot blame anyone outside of yourself.

Nothing is more important to us than our conception of ourselves, and this is especially true of our concept of the deep, dimensionally greater one within us. Those who help or hinder us, whether they know it or not, are the servants of that law, which shapes outward circumstances in harmony with our inner nature.

It is our conception of ourselves that either frees or constrains us, allowing it to use material agencies to achieve its purpose.

Life molds the outer world to reflect the inner arrangement of our minds; there is no way of bringing about perfection outside ourselves. We seek transformation not from external sources, but by changing ourselves. The hills we gaze upon lie within, beyond our conscious awareness, where we must turn to find the only reality.

It is the foundation upon which all phenomena can be explained, and we can rely absolutely on the justice of this law, receiving only that which is in line with our own nature. To attempt to change the world before changing our concept of ourselves is to struggle against the nature of things. There can be no outward change until an inner change is made, as within, so without.

There is nothing to change but our concept of self. As soon as we succeed in transforming self, our world will dissolve and reshape itself in harmony with that change. Affirming and dissenting consciousness have brought about the imperfection that I see. We cannot lose anything except by descent in consciousness from the sphere where the thing has its natural life.

Had I a noble, dignified concept of myself, I never could have seen the unlovely in others.

The invitation given to us in the Scriptures is to be absent from the body and be present with the Lord. The body is your former conception of yourself, and the Lord, your awareness of being.

This is what is meant when Jesus said to Nicodemus, 'Ye must be born again,' for except you be born again, you cannot enter the kingdom of heaven. That is, except you leave behind your present conception of yourself and assume the nature of the new birth, you will continue to out picture your present limitations.

You can only be to others what you are first to yourself; therefore, to revalue yourself and begin to feel yourself to be the giant, a centre of power, is to dwarf those former giants and make of them grasshoppers.

Revelation, 'I and my Father are one,' but 'my Father is greater than I,' means you are one with your present conception of yourself, but you are greater than that which you are presently aware of being.

As you meet people, they tell you by their behaviour who you are.

ASSUMPTION

An assumption brings the invisible into sight. It is nothing more nor less than seeing with the eye of God ie imagination.

The only fate governing your life is the faith, determined by your own concepts, your own assumptions, for an assumption, though false, if persisted in, will harden into fact, that which you will not affirm, as true of yourself, can never be realised by you, for that attitude, alone is the necessary condition by which you realise your goal.

If you and I could feel what it would be like to be that which we want to be and live in this mental atmosphere as though it were real, then, in a way we do not fully comprehend, our assumption would harden into fact. This is all we need to do in order to ascend to the level where our assumption is already an objective, concrete reality.

Feed the mind with premises that are assertions presumed to be true because assumptions, though false, if persisted in until they have the feeling of reality, will harden into fact.

Quietly, assume that you are that which you now want to be, and in a way, you do not know you will become it.

As I ascend in consciousness, the power and the glory that was mine return to me, and I too will say, 'I have finished the work which You gave me to do.' The work is to return from my descent in consciousness from the level where I believed that I was a son of man to the sphere where I know that I am one with my father, and my father is God.

If we walk as though we were already the ideal we serve, we will rise to the level of our assumption and find a world in harmony with our assumption. We will not have to lift a finger to make it so, for it is already so.

A change of assumption is a change of expression.

What it would be like to be what we desire and live in a mental atmosphere as though it were already real, then, in a mysterious way, our assumption would solidify into a concrete fact. This is the essential process we must undertake to elevate our assumption to the level where it becomes an objective reality, already existing in the physical world.

If the state desired is for yourself, and you find it difficult to accept as true, what your senses deny call before your minds eye the subjective image of a friend, and have him mentally affirm that you are already that which you desire to be. This establishes in him, without his conscious consent or knowledge, the subconscious assumption that you are that which he mentally affirmed. This assumption because it is unconsciously assumed will persist until it fulfils its mission. Its mission is to awaken in you the identical vibration.

THE BIBLE

To take the Bible away from its central idea of rebirth, which means an inner evolution and implies the existence of a higher level, is to understand nothing of its real meaning.

The word of God, that is, the psychological teaching in the Bible, is to make a man different first in thought, and then in being, so that he becomes a new man or is born again.

Blessed are the meek, for they shall inherit the Earth in the original text. The word translated as "meek" is the opposite of the words "resentful" and "angry." It means becoming tamed, as a wild animal is tamed. After the mind is tamed, it may be likened to a vine, of which it may be said, "Behold this vine, I found it a wild tree, whose wanton strength has swelled into irregular twigs. But I pruned the plant, which grew temperate, shedding its useless leaves and knotting into these clean, full clusters, to repay the hand that wisely wounded it."

The Bible is written in the language of symbolism. Its characteristics of personification are the laws and functions of mind. The Bible is psychology rather than history.

If you have listened carefully, you now know that the Bible has no reference to any persons that ever existed or to any events that ever occurred upon earth. The authors of the Bible were not writing history; they were writing a great drama of the mind, which they dressed up in the garb of history and then adapted it to the limited capacity of the uncritical thinking masses. The Bible is your story, and when the writers introduced thousands of characters in the same story, they were trying to present you with different attributes of the mind that you may employ.

To read and understand the Bible, one must be imaginatively awake.

In prayer, you are called upon to believe that you possess what your reason and your senses deny. When you pray, believe that you will receive, as the Bible states: "Therefore I say unto you, what things soever you desire when you pray, believe that you will receive them, and you shall have them. And when you stand praying, forgive, if you have anything against anyone, so that your Father also, who is in heaven, may forgive you your trespasses. But if you do not forgive, neither will your Father, who is in heaven, forgive your trespasses."

- Mark 11:24

PRAYER

Prayer, the art of believing what is denied by the senses, deals, almost entirely, with the subconscious.

Prayer is the feeling of the fulfilled desire.

Consciousness being God, one must seek in consciousness for the thing, desired by assuming the consciousness of the quality desired only as one does. This will help his prayers be answered.

Praying, then, is recognising yourself to be that which you desire to be rather than begging God for that which you desire.

It does not matter what it is you seek in prayer, or where it is, or whom it concerns you have nothing to do, but convince yourself of the truth of that which you desire to see manifested.

When you emerge from prayer, you no longer seek for you have, if you have prayed correctly, subconsciously assumed the reality of the state sought, and by the law of reversibility, your subconscious, must objectify that which it affirms.

Prayer is the most wonderful experience Man can have. Prayer is the ecstasy of a spiritual wedding, taking place in the deep, silent stillness of consciousness.

Prayers to be successful must be claimed and appropriated.

Assume the positive consciousness of the thing desired when you emerge from the hour of prayer. You must do so conscious of being and possessing what you heretofore desired.

Praying, as we have shown you before, is recognition in conjunction with the belief that you receive. It is first person present tense. This means that you must be in the nature of the things asked for before you can receive them. To get into the nature easily, general amnesty is necessary.

When you pray, go within in secret and shut the door. That which your Father sees in secret, with that, will He reward you openly. We have identified the Father to be the awareness of being. We have also identified the door to be the awareness of being. So, shutting the door is shutting out that which I am now aware of being and claiming myself to be that which I desire to be. The very moment my claim is established to the point of conviction, that moment I begin to draw onto myself the evidence of my claim. Do not question the how of these things appearing, for no man knows the way that is no manifestation knows how the things desired will appear.

Put yourself in the proper mood, and your own consciousness will embody it. If I could define prayer for anyone and put it as clearly as I could, I would simply say it is the feeling of the wish fulfilled. If you ask, "What do you mean by that?" I would say I would feel myself into the situation of the answered prayer, and then I would live and act upon that conviction. I will try to sustain it without effort. That is, I would live and act as though it were already a fact, knowing that as I walk in this fixed attitude, my vision will harden into reality.

THE FATHER

My father and I are one, but my father is greater than I ... The conscious and subconscious, are one, but the subconscious is greater than the conscious.

Our awareness is God, the Father, who holds the blueprint of the perfect directional vision. It reminds the child, 'My Father and I are one.' The child and the father are one.

Man's eternal journey serves one purpose: to reveal the Father. He comes to make his Father visible, and the Father's presence is evident in all the lovely things of this world.

Embrace the beautiful and positive aspects, having no time for the unlovely, regardless of what they may be. What you seek is already within you; without it, eternity could not evolve, as there would be no time long enough to develop what is not potentially involved in you. Simply allow it to come into being by assuming it is already visible in your world and remaining faithful to that assumption. It will solidify into reality. Your Father has countless ways of confirming your assumptions.

Keep this in mind and remember that an assumption, even if initially false, will harden into fact if sustained.

You and your Father are one, and your Father is everything that was, is, and will be. Therefore, that which you seek, you already are, and it can never be so far off as even to be near. The great Pascal said, "You never would have sought me had you not already found me." What you now desire, you already have, and you see, it's only because you have already found it. You found it in the form of desire. It is just as real in the form of desire as it is going to be to your bodily organs. You are already that which you seek, and you have no one to change but self in order to express it.

The feeling or thrill that comes to one in response to his self- questioning is the father state of consciousness or foundation stone upon which the consciousness change is built.

It is the awakening of the imagination, the return of his son, that our father waits for.

The Son is the idea and the Father is the actualisation of the idea. Therefore the idea and the promise of its actualisation or one the Father and the Son of one.

Father is God consciousness. The Father in scripture represents God consciousness. The I am presence the Shepherd.

Revelation, 'I and my Father are one,' but 'my Father is greater than I' means you are one with your present conception of yourself, but you are greater than that which you are presently aware of being.

The feeling or thrill that comes to one in response to his self- questioning is the father state of consciousness or the foundation stone upon which the consciousness change is built.

CHRIST

Did you know that the resurrection and crucifixion of Christ in the Easter story is symbolic of the death that we must all go through in order to birth our Christed self?

Christ is not to be found in history, nor in external forms. You find Christ only when you become aware of the fact that your imagination is the only redemptive power. When this is discovered, the towers of dogma will have heard the trumpets of truth and like the walls of Jericho crumble to dust.

Contemplate the ideal state and identify yourself with it, and you will ascend to the sphere where you, as Christ, have your natural life.

If thou canst believe:
all things are possible to him that believeth.

The birth of Christ is the awakening of the inner or second man.

Christ in you is your imagination.

MENTAL
CONVERSATIONS

It is not what you want that you attract. You attract what you believe to be true, therefore get into the spirit of these mental conversations and give them the same degree of reality that you would a telephone conversation.

Success is gained by inner talking.

Mentally talk to your friends as though your
desires for them were already realized.

What you sincerely believe as true of another you will awaken within him.

Represent the subject to yourself mentally, as though he had already done that which you desire him to do, mentally speak to him and congratulate him on having done what you want him to do mentally see him in the state you want him to obtain. Within the circle of its action, every word, subject to be spoken awakens, objectively, what it affirms, incredulity on the part of the subject, is no hindrance when you are in control of your every thought.

A very effective way to pray for oneself is to use the formula of Job. He found that his own captivity was removed as he prayed for his friends - fix your attention on a friend and have the imaginary voice of your friend tell you that he is or has that which is comparable to that which you desire to be or have. As you mentally hear and see him - feel the thrill of his good fortune and sincerely wish him well. This awakens in him, the corresponding vibration of the state affirmed, and this vibration must then objectify itself as a physical fact. You will discover the truth of the statement, "Blessed are the merciful, for they shall receive mercy." The quality of mercy is twice given.

An assumption brings the invisible into sight. It is nothing more nor less than seeing with the eye of God ie imagination.

The Subconscious Mind

Control of the subconscious is dominion over all.

The little flower which has bloomed once blooms forever. It is invisible to you here with your limited focus, but it blooms forever in the larger dimension of your being, and tomorrow you will encounter it.

As a man thinketh in his heart in the deep subconscious of himself, so is he.

DESIRE

The object of your desire is never far off. Its intense nearness makes it remote from observation of the senses. It dwells in consciousness, and consciousness is closer than breathing and nearer than hands and feet.

Knowing that your awareness is God, you should look upon its desire as the spoken word of God.

All that you could ever desire is already present and only waiting to be matched by your beliefs.

A most effective way to embody a desire is to assume the feeling of the wish fulfilled, and then in a relaxed and sleepy state, repeat over and over again, the lullaby or any short phrase which implies the fulfilment of your desire, such as "thank you, thank you, thank you," until the single sensation of thankfulness dominates the mind. Speak these words as though you addressed a Higher Power for doing it for you.

Your desire, though invisible, must be affirmed by you to be something real.

Until his whole self thrills with the feeling of actually being his conscious claim and consciously living in the state of being it, only in this way, will man ever resurrect, or realise his desires.

Secrecy is the first law to be observed in realising your desire.

The reason most of us fail to realise our desires is that we are constantly conditioning them. Do not condition your desire; just accept it as it comes to you. Give thanks for it to the point that you are grateful for having already received it, then go about your way in peace.

Acceptance of your desire is like dropping a fertile seed into prepared soil. When you can drop the thing desired into consciousness, confident that it shall appear, you have done all that is expected of you.

But to be worried or concerned about your desire maturing is to hold these fertile seeds in a mental grasp and, therefore, never to have dropped them into the soil of confidence.

We must fish in consciousness for the things that we desire. We must only ever fish in the deep waters of consciousness.

COMPILED BY JEN MCCARTY

If you were accustomed to great accomplishments, you would give yourself a much shorter interval in which to accomplish your desire.

Merge yourself in the feeling of being that which you desire, whether it's an old or newly attained consciousness. Only by embodying the feeling of the newly attained consciousness can you know who you truly are. Its ways are past finding out, so do not speculate with this consciousness, for no man, is wise enough to know.

Speculation is proof that you have not attained the naturalness of being the same as desired, and so you are filled with doubts.

If you have not the consciousness of the thing, you have not the cause or foundation upon which the thing is erected. A proof of this established consciousness is given to you in the words, 'Thank you, Father,' when you come into the joy of thanksgiving so that you feel grateful for having received that which is not yet apparent to the senses. You have become one in consciousness with the thing for which you gave thanks.

Faith is now the substance which clothes your desire as it's rising in consciousness. The spiritual marriage wherein you shall agree upon being one, and their likeness or image is established on Earth, for whatsoever you ask in my name, the same give I am to you.

Your dimensionally larger self speaks to you through the language of desire. Do not deceive yourself; knowing what you want, claim that you already have it, for it is your Father's good pleasure to give it to you. And remember, what you desire, you have.

Man, by assuming the feelings of his wish fulfilled, and then living and acting on this conviction, alters the future in harmony with his assumptions. As soon as Man assumes the feeling of his wish fulfilled, his fourth-dimensional self paves the way for the attainment of this end and discovers methods for its realization.

BELIEF

In consciousness, all states exist objectively and are awakened to their objective existence by belief.

To him that hath it shall be given.

The moment man matches the beliefs of any state, he fuses with it, and this union results in the activation and projection of its plots, plans, dramas, and situations.

It is no effort for me to conjure poverty if I am conscious of being poor.

Just how this feeling will embody itself, no one knows, but it will.

The moment man matches the beliefs of any state, he fuses with it, and this union results in the activation and projection of its plots, plans, dramas, and situations.

If you see it has been done, it is done.

The thieves who rob you are your own false beliefs. It is your belief in a thing, not the thing itself, that aids you. There is only one power, 'I am he.' Because of your belief in external things, you think power into them by transferring the power that you are to the external thing.

Realise yourself as all the power you have mistakenly given to outer conditions.

The state becomes the individual's home, from which he views the world. It is his workshop, and if he is observant, he will see his outer reality shaping itself upon the model of his imagination.

Before mankind attempts to transform his world, he must first lay the foundation. I am the Lord; that is man's awareness.

His consciousness of being is God. Until this is firmly established, so that no suggestion or argument put forward by others can shake it, he will find himself returning to the slavery of his former beliefs.

THINKING FROM
THE END

Don't think of your ideal think from it.
It is only the ideals from which you think
that are ever realized.

Thinking from the end is the way of Christ.

You must imagine yourself into the state of your wish fulfilled, and in so doing, live and think from it, and no more of it, you pass from thinking of to thinking from by centring your imagination in the feeling of the wish fulfilled.

Until his whole self thrills with the feeling of actually being his conscious claim and consciously living in the state of being it, only in this way will man ever resurrect or realise his desires.

We must use imagination masterfully, not as an onlooker thinking of the end, but as a partaker thinking from the end.
We must actually be there in imagination. If we do this, our subjective experience will be realized objectively.

MENTAL DIET

By a change of mental diet you can alter the course of observed events, but unless there is a change of mental diet, your personal history remains the same.

You cannot put new wine in old bottles or new patches on old garments. That is, you cannot take with you into the new consciousness any part of the old man, all of your present beliefs, fears, and limitations are weights that bind you to your present level of consciousness.

If you would transcend this level, you must leave behind all that is now your present self or conception of yourself. To do this, you take your attention away from all that is now your problem or limitation and dwell upon just being.

FAITH

Tell no man of your spiritual romance. Lock your secret within you, enjoy it confidently, and be happy that someday you will be the son of your lover by expressing and possessing the nature of your impression.

To him that hath it shall be given.

The only fate governing your life is the faith, determined by your own concepts, your own assumptions, for an assumption, though false, if persisted in, will harden into fact, that which you will not affirm, as true of yourself, can never be realised by you, for that attitude, alone is the necessary condition by which you realise your goal.

If you walk faithful to a high mood, there will be no opposition and no competition. The strange thing is that as we keep the high mood and do not fall off this cushion, the world will spread the palm leaves before us to cushion our journey. We do not have to be concerned about shocks, as they will be softened as we move into the fulfillment of our desire. Our high mood awakens in others the ideas and actions which tend towards the embodiment of our mood. If we walk faithful to a high mood, there will be no opposition and no competition.

Doubt is the only force capable of disturbing the seed or impression, to avoid a miscarriage of so wonderful a child. It walks in secrecy through the necessary interval of time for the impression to become an expression.

Problems are the mountains spoken of that can be moved if everyone has, but the faith of a grain of a mustard seed.

The habit of saying only that which our senses permit renders us totally blind to what otherwise we could see. To cultivate the faculty of seeing the invisible, we should often deliberately disentangle our minds from the evidence of the senses and focus our attention on an invisible state, mentally feeding and sensing it until it has all the distinctness of reality.

You would not have sought me had you not already found me?

Do you not be anxious or concerned as to results they will follow just as surely as the day follows the night.

INNER SELF

The door of the senses must be tightly shut
before your new claim can be honoured.

Unless I am conscious of being that which I seek I will not find it.

Creation is finished. You call your creation into being by feeling the reality of the state you desire.

To passively surrender to the evidence of the senses underestimates the capacity of the inner self.

Unless I am conscious of being that which I seek I will not find it.

Man must firmly come to believe that reality lies within him, and not without. Although others have bodies and lives of their own, their reality is rooted in you, just as yours ends in God.

That is, you say silently but feelingly to yourself, 'I am not conditioning this awareness as yet.' Just declare yourself to be, and continue to do so until you are lost in the feeling of just being, faceless and formless. When this expansion of consciousness is attained, then within this formless deep of yourself, give form to the new conception by feeling yourself to be that which you desire to be.

You will find within this deep of yourself all things to be divinely possible. Everything in the world which you can conceive of being is, to you, within this present formless awareness, a most natural attainment.

SABBATH

The sabbath follows this crucifixion or fixation of the new conscious claim. A time of rest.

There is always an interval of time between the impressions, and the expression between the conscious claim, and its embodiment. This interval is called the sabbath period of rest or non-effort, the day of entombment to walk in, moving in the consciousness of being or possessing a certain state is to keep the sabbath. When the new state of consciousness is appropriated, so you feel, by this appropriation, fixed and secure in the knowledge that it is finished.

You two will cry out it is finished and will enter the tomb or sabbath, an interval in which you will walk on moved in the conviction that your new consciousness must be resurrected and made visible.

How to manifest anything: first, define your objective, not the manner of obtaining it, but your objective, pure and simple know exactly what it is you desire so that you have a clear mental picture of it. Secondly, take your attention away from the obstacles, which separate you from your objective and place your thoughts on the objective itself, thirdly, close your eyes, and feel that you are already in the city or state that you would be in upon the realisation of your goal, and remain within this psychological state, until you get a conscious reaction of complete satisfaction in this victory, then by simply opening your eyes return to your former, conscious state. This secret of journeying into the desired state with its subsequent psychological reaction of complete satisfaction is all that is necessary to bring about the victory. This victorious physical state will embody itself despite all opposition.

You, who know this law, will find that after capturing the psychological state which would be yours if you were already victoriously and actually entrenched in that city or state, you will move towards the physical realisation of your desires. You will do this without doubt or fear, in a state of mind fixed in the knowledge of a pre-arranged victory.

I AM

The whole world is waiting for you to claim I am.

The whole world is waiting for you to embody your I am presence.

When you say 'I am,' you are declaring yourself to be in the first person present tense.

There is no future. To know that 'I am' is to be conscious of being. Consciousness is the only door.

Unless you are conscious of being that which you seek, you seek in vain. If you judge after appearances, you will continue to be enslaved by the evidence of your senses.

In other words, awareness is the Shepherd and the sheep always follow the Shepherd. The sheep represent the lower third-dimensional world, which must stand in accordance with the I am presence. The Shepherd is awareness/the I am presence.

In your formless awareness, lies buried all that you will ever conceive yourself to be. Your claim that you are now that which you want to be, will remove the veil of human darkness and reveal your claim perfectly.
I am that.

Your awareness of being is Lord and Shepherd of your life. 'The Lord is my shepherd; I shall not want' is seen in its true light now to be your consciousness.

'The Lord is my shepherd; I shall not want' means the Lord, the governor of my consciousness, is my I am presence. When I am at one with my I am presence, I shall not want for anything, because within the I am presence, I possess all. It is just as easy to possess the consciousness of negative qualities as it is to possess the opposite.

If you believe not that I am He, you shall die in your sins. That is, you shall continue to be confused and thwarted until you find the cause of your confusion. When you have lifted up the Son of Man, then shall you know that I am He, that is, that I, John Smith, do nothing of myself, but my Father or that state of consciousness which I am now one with does the works.

Consciousness is the way/order through which things appear. He said, 'I am the way,' not 'I, John Smith, am the way,' but 'I am the awareness of being,' is the way through which the theme shall come. The signs always follow; they never proceed. Things have no reality other than in consciousness; therefore, get the consciousness first, and the thing is compelled to appear.

GOD

The one and only God is your awareness.

Then you will know the mystery of God, who said, 'Let us make man in our image.' You will know that the reality of gods refers to the three aspects of your own consciousness and that you are the Trinity meeting in a spiritual conclave to fashion a world in the image and likeness of that which you are conscious of being.

The Father, Son and Holy Spirit are three aspects for conditions of the unconditioned awareness of being called God.

Man must see this story of the virgin birth as a psychological drama rather than a statement of physical fact. In so doing, he will discover the Bible to be based on the law, which, when self-applied, will result in a manifested expression transcending his wildest dreams of accomplishment. To apply this law of self-expression, man must be schooled in the belief and disciplined to stand upon the platform that all things are possible to God.

You have become so invested in the belief that you are man that you have forgotten the glorious being that you are. Now, with your memory restored, decree the unseen to appear, and it shall appear. All things are compelled to respond to the voice of God, your awareness of being. The world is at your command.

CONSCIOUSNESS

Consciousness is the reality that eternally solidifies itself in the things around you. Man's world, in its every detail, is his consciousness out pictured.

Consciousness is the only true foundation in the world.

There is no reality in the world other than your consciousness.

When you say 'I am,' you are declaring yourself to be in the first person present tense. There is no future. To know that 'I am' is to be conscious of being.
Consciousness is the only door.
Unless you are conscious of being that which you seek, you seek in vain. If you judge after appearances, you will continue to be enslaved by the evidence of your senses.
Consciousness is the only reality, and things but mirror that which you are in consciousness.
So, the heavenly state you are seeking will be found only in consciousness, for the kingdom of heaven is within you.

I by my descent in consciousness to a lower level, causing these things to disappear from my sight, and I say they have gone, they are finished as far as my world goes. All I need to do is ascend to the level where they are eternal, and they once more objectify themselves and appear as realities within my world.

And for there is no clear conception of the origin of phenomena, except that consciousness is all, and all is consciousness.

BRIDE AND GROOM

In its true sense, prayer is Gods marriage ceremony, just as a maid on her wedding day, is the name of her family, to assume the name of her husband in like manner, one who praises must relinquish his present, name or nature, and assume the nature of that which he prays.

Going within is the entering of the bridal chamber, just as no one but the bride and groom is permitted to enter so holy a room as the bridal suite on the night of the marriage ceremony.

Likewise, no one but the one who prays and that for which he prays is permitted to enter the holy hour of prayer. As the bride and groom, on entering the bridal suite, securely shut the door against the outside world, so too must the one who enters the holy hour of prayer close the door of the senses and entirely shut out the world around about him.

SHEPHERD

The Everlasting Father is your awareness of being well. I am the Good Shepherd, and I know my sheep, and they are known of mine. My sheep hear my voice, and I know them, and they will follow me. Awareness is the Good Shepherd; what I am aware of being is the sheep that follow me. So, as a Good Shepherd, your awareness has never lost one of the sheep that you are aware of being.

In other words, awareness is the Shepherd and the sheep always follow the Shepherd. The sheep represent the lower third-dimensional world, which must stand in accordance with the I am presence. The Shepherd is awareness/the I am presence.

Discipline/ Meekness

A meek man is a self-disciplined man. He is so disciplined; he sees only the finest. He thinks only the best. He is the one who fulfils the suggestion: "Brother, whatsoever things are true, whatsoever things are honest, whatsoever things are just, whatsoever things are pure, whatsoever things are lovely, whatsoever things are of good report, if there be any virtue, and if there be any praise, think on these things."

In truth, a meek man is a man in complete control of his moods, and his moods are the highest, for he knows, he must keep a high mood if he would walk with the highest.

A suggestion of lack could never pass the watch of the disciplined mind of the mystic, for he knows that every conscious claim must in time be expressed as a condition of the world of his environment, so he remains faithful to his beloved, his defined objective by defining and claiming himself to be, that which he desires to express, let a man ask himself if his defined objective would be a thing of joy and beauty if it were realized.

A disciplined mind is emphasised in the Bible. Jesus uses the analogy of riding a young, unbridled horse to convey this message.

The young horse represents the new desire, which requires mental discipline to fulfil one's desires safely. Likewise, the young horse symbolises the monkey mind, which can be tamed through consistency and discipline.

A fixed attitude of mind, a feeling that it is done, will make it so. If I walk as though it were, but every once in a while, I look to see if it is, then I fall off my mood or my colt.

FINAL SECTION

There is no escape from our present predicament except by a radical psychological transformation everything depends upon our attitude towards ourselves that which we will not affirm as true of ourselves will not develop in our lives.

All of us must learn to ride the animal straight into Jerusalem, the city of peace, unassisted by a man. We do not need another to help us.

He who practices these exercises of bi-location will develop unusual powers of concentration and quiescence, and will inevitably achieve waking consciousness of the inner and dimensionally larger world.

If you do not condemn yourself, there will be no one in your world to condemn you. If you are living in the consciousness of your ideal, you will see nothing to condemn.

The state becomes the individual's home, from which he views the world. It is his workshop, and if he is observant, he will see our reality shaping itself upon the model of his imagination.

Far greater is he that is in you than he that is in the world.

If we would become as emotionally aroused over our ideas as we become over our dislikes, we would ascend to the plane of our ideal as easily as we now descend to the level of our habits.

There is no way to bring about the perfection we seek other than by transforming ourselves. As soon as we succeed in transforming ourselves, the world will melt magically before our eyes, and reshape itself in harmony with that which our transformation firms.

The subjective mind is the diffused consciousness that animates the world. It is the spirit that giveth life.

To change the conditions here in the three dimensions of space, we must first change them in the four dimensions of space.

Try as Man will, he cannot find a course of manifestation other than his consciousness of being.

The mouth of God is the mind of man.

Creation is finished. You call your creation
into being by feeling the reality of the state
you desire.

A mood attracts its affinities.

Man, in his blindness, will not hear the prophet's advice. He continues to label himself as weak, poor, wretched, and all other undesirable expressions, from which he is trying to free himself. He ignorantly claims that he will be free from these characteristics in the future. Such thoughts, though, thwart the one law that can ever free him.

Take no thought of tomorrow, tomorrow's expressions are determined by today's impressions.

Matching the beliefs of a state is the seeking that finds and the asking that receives.

All outward appearances are but states of mind externalized.

I am and the world is the mirror magnifying all that I am conscious of being. Man's attempt to change the world by force is as fruitless as breaking a mirror in the hope of changing his face.

Leave the mirror and change your face.

Leave the world alone, and change your conceptions of yourself.

It is, for this purpose of training us in image-making, that we were made subject to the limitations of the senses and clothed in bodies of flesh.

You must stop looking for your saviour to appear and begin claiming that you are already saved. The signs of your claims will follow your awareness, magnifying your consciousness.

To claim that you shall have joyful oil is to confess that you have empty measures. Such impressions of lack produce lack.

Forgiveness is experiencing, in imagination, the revised version of the day; experiencing in imagination what you wish you had experienced in the flesh. Every time one really forgives, we live the event as it should have been lived.

TECHNIQUE

Neville recommends that you put yourself in a drowsy state every day at the same time. Make sure you are very, very comfortable and relaxed, and set a specific time commitment every day. You will notice that as that time comes, you will begin to feel drowsy.

One of the most fundamental requisites, with regards to the technique, is to arouse your attention in a way and to such intensity that you become holy absorbed in the revised action, you will experience an expansion of refinement of the senses through this imaginative, exercise, and eventually achieve the vision.

Construct mentally a drama which implies that your desire is realised. Make it one that involves movement of self, as though you were going to take a nap, and start the predetermined action in your imagination. Create a vivid representation of the action, imagining the beginning of that action. As you are falling asleep, consciously place yourself into the scene. The length of sleep is not important; a short nap is sufficient to carry the action into sleep. This process thickens fancy into fact. At first, it might feel like rambling sheep without a shepherd. Don't despair if your attention strays; bring it back to its predetermined course until exhaustion leads it to follow the appointed path.

The inner journey must never be without direction. When you take to the inner road, do what you did mentally before you started. Go for the prize you have already seen and accepted.

Now, what do I want? I must define my objective. For example, suppose I wanted to be elsewhere at this very moment. I desire to be elsewhere. I need not go through the door, I need not sit down, I need to do nothing but stand just where I am. With my eyes closed, I assume I am standing where I desire to be. Then I remain in this state until it has the feeling of reality, where I know elsewhere, I could not see the world as I now see it from here. The world changes in its relationship to me as I change my position in space.

So I stand right here, close my eyes, and imagine I am seeing what I would see were I out there. I remain in it long enough to feel it to be real. I cannot touch the walls of this room from here, but when you close your eyes and become still, you can imagine and feel that you touch it. You can stand where you are and imagine you are putting your hand on the wall to prove you are. Put it there and slide it up and feel the wall. You can imagine you are doing it without getting off your seat. You can do it, and you will feel it if you become still enough and intense enough.

To manifest anything, first, define your objective clearly and simply, focusing on what you desire without worrying about how. Create a vivid mental picture of your objective in your mind. Secondly, shift your attention away from the obstacles that may separate you from your objective.

Instead, direct your thoughts and energy towards the objective itself. Thirdly, close your eyes and immerse yourself in already being in the city or state you desire to manifest. Stay in this psychological state until you feel a conscious reaction of complete satisfaction in achieving this victory. After experiencing the satisfaction, simply open your eyes and return to your usual conscious state. This secret journey into the desired state and the subsequent feeling of satisfaction is all that is necessary to bring about the manifestation of your objective. Trust that this victorious mental and emotional state will embody itself despite any opposition, as you tap into the plan and power of self- expression within you.

We have now reached the end of this powerful book of quotations from the wonderful mystic, Neville Goddard. I highly recommend reading this book from cover to cover, and I recommend opening up this book randomly throughout your day to align with messages from your subconscious mind. The only way to test whether these teachings work is to try them out.

Do your best to deeply embody the powerful reminders that are offered in this book of Neville's quotations. Please know you have my deepest love with you on your journey of becoming a master manifester, and please know that the whole universe is uplifted when we can harness the power of our subconscious mind and manifest the life of our dreams.

I will conclude this book of quotations by sharing, in-depth, Neville's suggestion on precisely how to work with the technique.

THE TECHNIQUE

Neville's prayer technique involves finding a comfortable armchair and lying flat on his back. He ensures his body is deeply relaxed, which marks the first stage of prayer and knowing what he desires. Next, he constructs a simple event in his mind that implies realising his desire and exploring various possibilities before settling on the most likely outcome.

Once he decides on the action that implies fulfilment, Neville sits or lies down comfortably, closing his eyes to induce a drowsy state bordering on sleep. He knows he's in the perfect condition for successful prayer when he feels this state or a sense of togetherness.

In this state, he takes the restricted action representing the fulfilment of his prayer, fully immersing himself in the experience as if he were an actor playing a part. Rather than merely visualizing, Neville physically engages with the imagined action.

He envisions his greater self coming out of his body and performing the desired action. Whether walking, climbing stairs, or shaking hands, he feels and acts it out within his imagination.

Neville acknowledges that this controlled daydreaming is an actual act in the greater dimension of his being, transcending the limitations of three- dimensional space.

He adopts a feeling of thankfulness, implying the realisation of his desires, and assumes the sensation of the wish fulfilled before going to sleep. Entering a drowsy state without effort, Neville lets a single sense dominate his mind during successful prayer. He focuses on how he would feel if his desires were already fulfilled, losing himself in that sensation.

In doing so, Neville believes that his dimensionally greater self constructs a bridge of incidents, guiding him from the present moment towards fulfilling his desires. And that's all one needs to do to employ this technique successfully.

LEARN MORE ABOUT THE AUTHOR, JEN MCCARTY

SCAN ME